MODERN AMERICAN ETCHERS
ARTHUR WILLIAM HEINTZELMAN

ARTHUR WILLIAM HEINTZELMAN

FOREWORD
AND
CRITICAL NOTES BY
JOHN TAYLOR ARMS

MINTON, BALCH & COMPANY ～ NEW YORK

FOREWORD

PROPHECIES are always dangerous, particularly when they apply to the future standing of contemporary artists, yet it seems safe to say that the work of Arthur William Heintzelman is destined to occupy a high place in the realm of etching. Though he is but a young man, on the very threshold of his professional career, his reputation is already firmly established on both sides of the Atlantic, and examples of his art are eagerly sought for, both by private buyers and by the great national collections. His rise to eminence has been rapid indeed, but it has none the less resulted from a normal and healthy artistic growth, and no one who has followed it year by year can question the lasting quality of the foundations on which it is built. Many a man who is merely clever, or who has the wit or good fortune to stumble upon subject matter that has a popular appeal, comes rapidly to the fore in public attention, only to sink out of sight as quickly when it becomes apparent that his work lacks those enduring qualities which are so essential to all true artistic expression.

Heintzelman has not sought the quick road to success, but rather has he approached his art with all the seriousness of the student and the thinker. In these days, when craftsmanship as the masters knew it, is almost unknown, he has spent years in mastering the technical secrets of what is probably the most exacting of all the graphic media, until today he stands untrammeled by the difficulties which beset so many men who have endeavored to express their ideas before they have acquired more than a mere working vocabulary. No lover of the engraver's art can study the etchings of Heintzelman without at once realizing that here is a man who, when he undertakes a plate, knows exactly what he wishes to do, and, knowing this, is perfectly equipped to do it. Such a sure and accomplished touch as his every production vouchsafes, can only come with technical knowledge which is the fruit of long study and experiment. Nor is the beauty of the work the result simply of dexterity with the needle and acid, for the spiritual element is ever present as well, dominating each stroke, and imbuing the whole with both a strength and a grace that the hand alone cannot impart. There have been great technicians who lacked artistry, and very real artists who were deficient in technical accomplishment, but in each case something has been lacking. In Heintzelman, we find that rare and happy combination of the artist and the craftsman, the one supplying the conception, the other offering the means of expressing it in terms of beauty and lucidity.

Masters are rare, and seldom established except with the help of that perspective which time alone can give, yet we recognize in Heintzelman a man in whose oeuvre is evidenced a very high order of artistic merit, combined with a thorough knowledge of the particular medium he has chosen to make his own. Dangerous though it may be to make prophecies, the writer cannot but believe that this man is destined to go far indeed, a belief which is bound to be strengthened and enhanced by the undeniable quality of what the artist has already accomplished in his elected field.

JOHN TAYLOR ARMS

Fairfield, Connecticut
July, 1927

CHRONOLOGICAL LIST OF ETCHINGS

		Size in inches	Edition
— 1915 —			
1.	The Rabbi	5 x 3	50
2.	The Balloon Man	4 x 2½	50
3.	A Market Woman	4 x 2¾	50
4.	The Crucifix	5 x 3	2
— 1916 —			
5.	The Story Teller	5 x 3	4
6.	Fenner's Pond	6 x 5	3
7.	The Philosopher	6 x 5	5
8.	Head Study (small)	5 x 4	3
9.	Mr. Tingley	9 x 7	7
10.	Draped Head (large)	8 x 7	5
11.	Louis Welt	6½ x 4½	1
12.	Baby Cranston	6½ x 4½	10
— 1917 —			
13.	Mary Katherine	5 x 3	6
14.	A Landscape	4 x 3	4
15.	A Landscape	4 x 3	5
16.	The Fur Hat	5 x 4	3
17.	Winter	2½ x 4	6
18.	An Italian Woman	7 x 6	4
19.	Draped Head (small)	4 x 3	50
20.	Abdullah	7 x 6	20
21.	Knitting	5¾ x 5	25
22.	An Old Man Thinking	4½ x 3½	30
23.	Sands at Russell's Island	5 x 4	60
24.	The Violinist	3½ x 5½	50
25.	Heads (Etched on Zinc)	3¾ x 2½	20
26.	David	5½ x 4½	20
27.	The Guitar Player	8 x 6½	50
— 1918 —			
28.	Cranston	5 x 4	1
29.	Dorothy	5 x 3½	22
30.	An Old Fisherman	5 x 4	3
31.	The Fishing Wharf	5 x 4	4
32.	The Launching	4½ x 6	6
33.	The Artist	5½ x 4½	50
34.	The Black Hat	6 x 4½	50
35.	Leisure	7¼ x 5	50
36.	Contemplation	5⅜ x 3⅜	10
37.	Nude on Rocks	8 x 5	10
38.	Head with Black Drape	5 x 4	75
39.	A Country Blacksmith	5½ x 4½	50
40.	Head Study	8 x 5½	60
41.	Weighing Fish	4 x 5	25
42.	The Boat Builder	5 x 4	25
43.	The Pixie Baby	5 x 6¾	50
44.	Portrait of an Old Woman	2¾ x 2¼	50
45.	A Strolling Musician of Gloucester	8 x 6	75
— 1919 —			
46.	Medeo	8 x 6	25
47.	On the Old Magnolia Road	5 x 4	50
48.	Annisquam River from Babson's Hill	8 x 6	40
49.	In The Twilight	6¾ x 5½	50
50.	The Sun Bath	6 x 8	75
51.	The Squall	4½ x 5½	50
52.	Old White Horse	5 x 4	50
53.	Cows on the Moors	4 x 5	50
54.	High Pastures	4 x 5	50
55.	Youth and Old Age	5½ x 7¼	75
56.	A Sultry Afternoon	8 x 5½	75
57.	Early Morning Along the Shore	5½ x 4½	50
58.	Old Brass	6½ x 5	50
59.	The Walrus	6½ x 5	50
60.	Three Score and Ten	10½ x 8½	100
61.	The Pilgrim	7⅞ x 5⅞	100
62.	The Rehearsal	9⅞ x 8	100
63.	Portrait Study of an Old Man	5¾ x 4¾	100
— 1920 —			
64.	Study of Mother and Child	8 x 9	25
65.	Gloucester Fisherman	4⅜ x 2⅞	20

		Size in inches	Edition
— 1920 Continued **—**			
66.	Cow and Young Calf	5 x 7	10
67.	Old Man in Italian Cap (Plate for Brooklyn Society of Etchers)	8⅞ x 6⅞	250
68.	The Little Gamin	2¾ x 4¼	40
69.	Plate for The Print Connoisseur	4⅜ x 3⅜	
— 1921 —			
70.	Marchande de Café au Lait	8¾ x 8	100
— 1922 —			
71.	Merci	5¼ x 6	90
72.	Grand'mère Forain	8½ x 11¾	90
73.	Rolande	8½ x 11¾	100
74.	La Paysanne de Saint Germain	8 x 8½	90
75.	Freddie — "Café Lapin Agile"	5⅞ x 6	100
76.	Little Head, No. 1	2½ x 3¼	50
— 1923 —			
77.	La Boutique d'un Antiquaire	5⅝ x 6¾	60
78.	Edouard — Musicien Montmartrois	9¾ x 11⅜	115
79.	Hors de Service	3¾ x 5½	50
80.	Une Paysanne de Cayeux — Somme	5 x 6	50
81.	Une Propriétaire de Cayeux — Somme	4 x 5	100
82.	Bébé Malcolm	5 x 6¾	40
83.	Mother and Child	7¾ x 7¾	90
84.	Little Head, No. 2	3¼ x 3¾	100
85.	Donkey Cart in Montmartre (Plate for Chicago Society of Etchers)	7½ x 9½	300
86.	Little Head, No. 3 — Study for Merci	2⅞ x 2¼	100
87.	La Poissonnerie	8¼ x 9¼	75
88.	Objets d'Art	6¼ x 9½	70
89.	The Shawl	11⅝ x 8⅞	80
— 1924 —			
90.	The Poet — Bookplate for Mr. and Mrs. Armitt Brown	4 x 3⅛ before letters	24
91.	Crucifix (large)	11 x 9⅜	80
92.	L'Ouvrier	3⅝ x 2¾	100
93.	Un Mendiant	2⅞ x 2⅜	130
94.	Un Pêcheur de St. Valéry	3 x 2¼	130
95.	Sur la Place du Marché — St. Valéry	4⅞ x 5¼	80
96.	Crucifix (small)	8½ x 5⅞	60
— 1925 —			
97.	Plate for Société Gravure en Noir (programme)	6⅞ x 5¼	200
98.	Le Russe	3¾ x 2⅞	100
99.	Le Simple	3½ x 2⅞	60
100.	Etudes d'un Poète	5 x 4	100
101.	Planche aux Cinq Croquis	4⅛ x 5⅝	70
102.	Mater Dolorosa	7 x 4⅜	80
103.	Les Trois Maries	11⅜ x 7⅞	60
104.	Golgotha	15½ x 11	90
105.	Café Montmartrois	10 x 13¾	100
106.	Mise au Tombeau	7⅞ x 10⅞	50
107.	Etude d'un Artiste	3⅛ x 2½	70
— 1926 —			
108.	Mendiant — Italien	9⅝ x 6¾	1
109.	Prélude	9½ x 10½	115
110.	Chanteur Populaire	11 x 8	115
111.	Balayeuse	3⅞ x 3⅛	115
112.	Gamin de Borgio	9 x 7⅝	80
113.	Maternité	8½ x 6½	80
114.	Pierrot	8¼ x 5⅝	70
115.	Le Chevrier	7¾ x 9½	80
116.	Sculpteur de Pise	9 x 6½	100
117.	Vieille Femme de Sestri Levante	9½ x 6⅜	80
118.	Tendeur de Chèvres	4¾ x 3⅞	100
119.	Paysanne Endormie	9½ x 7⅛	80
120.	Convalescence	12 x 9¼	80
121.	Famille Suisse	9⅞ x 7¼	80
122.	Maria	2¾ x 2⅜	100
123.	Le Jeune Berger — Suisse	7 x 5	1

A Selection
from the Etchings of
ARTHUR WILLIAM HEINTZELMAN

Threescore and Ten. One of the artist's earlier plates, and one of his finest. The modeling of the face is magnificent, yet none of the strength and simplicity of the expression is lost by the intricacy of the detail. The cursory but masterly suggestion of the drapery, and of the body beneath it, is entirely adequate, and assists in concentrating the interest on the features above. The design of the whole is nobly conceived and beautifully executed.

Arthur Wm. Heintzelman

Chanteur Populaire. A recent plate, and an admirable bit of characterization. There is greater freedom in the drawing than in the earlier work, and the detail is everywhere felt, even when not actually expressed. The handling of the background is very successful, and aids materially in the illumination of the subject. Note the grace with which the hands are drawn and yet the strength they express.

Arthur W. F. Heintzelman

The Poet. This is, in the opinion of the writer, the finest thing Heintzelman has yet done. The manner of its production was remarkable. The subject was observed by the artist one evening in a Paris café, and the drawing was made then and there on a grounded plate the latter happened to have in his pocket. In order not to attract the attention of his sitter, Heintzelman held the plate, while he drew, on his knee, under the edge of the table at which he sat. The whole work occupied little more than half an hour, and the drawing was not subsequently altered in any way, except for the addition of a few lines on the left cheek. This exemplifies, to a telling degree, the artist's perfect control of his needle, and the sureness of his drawing.

Arthur Wm. Heintzelman

Motherhood. As full of grace and charm, as "Threescore and Ten" is of strength and power. The interplay of the lines of the composition is rhythmic and harmonious, and the drawing of the baby's head and hands is particularly beautiful. Though the artist's most distinguished work has perhaps been in the portrayal of old age, this plate goes to show that he can, when occasion demands, express the soft contours of youth with equal success.

Arthur Wm. Heintzelman

Maternité. Like the preceding one, this plate is distinguished by the tenderness of the feeling which pervades it. The universal appeal of the subject-matter, and the beauty of the design, combined with the delicacy of the actual drawing, unite to achieve a most appealing result. Note how successfully the artist has woven the dark notes afforded by the hair of the mother and the baby into his picture, by means of the long flowing lines of the drapery.

Mater Dolorosa. One of the most beautiful of the Biblical subjects. The pyramidal design is very effective, though at no point too obvious. Here everything is subordinated to the face of the Saviour, and upon this Heintzelman has lavished all his art. The rich burr of the drypoint has been used very tellingly in this plate to afford a series of staccato accents which lead up everywhere to the central point of interest. It is worthy of note that all of the artist's plates of religious subjects were etched before he visited the galleries of Italy, and studied the numerous works based on similar themes which are housed therein.

Golgotha. Whatever may be our opinion of Heintzelman's conception of the Crucifixion, it cannot be denied that it is fraught with great dignity and sincerity. In this day and generation, few artists turn to the Scriptures for their inspiration, and fewer still have chosen for a subject the most tragic and dramatic moment in human history. It would be hard to imagine anything more difficult to do, for here we see depicted the scene to the portrayal of which the greatest masters have brought, in a reverent and humble spirit, their supreme powers. That Heintzelman has succeeded in rendering the subject with dignity, is in itself a justification of the attempt. As always, his work is characterized by fine composition, and distinguished execution.

Café Montmartrois. A scene in the famous "Lapin Agile," one of the oldest of Montmartre cafés, and one whose presiding genius, "Freddie," is familiar to every art student of Paris. Heintzelman has undertaken a difficult task in this plate, and the success of his scheme of lighting is questionable. As a picture, there is a certain lack of cohesion in the elements which go to make it up, but as a study of individual portraits it is most interesting. "Freddie" himself is playing the cello, while the head to the right and in the rear of the dancing girl, is very reminiscent of the "Poet." There is never any hesitation about Heintzelman's work, and this composition, though it is perhaps not one of his best, is nevertheless rendered with a firmness and decision that preclude the possibility of any uncertainty in the artist's mind.

Objets d'Art. A plate that will be dear to all lovers of old Paris. Contrary to his usual custom, the artist has here subordinated the figure to its environment and in doing so, has proved that he can hold his own with the best of the etchers of quaint architectural fragments. Each individual bit of bric-a-brac in the heterogeneous mass that encumbers the sidewalk in front of the shop, is drawn with loving care, yet each takes its proper place in the scheme as a whole. The plate is finely balanced, and the transition from the highly finished detail in the center, to the lightly suggested objects at the edges, is subtle and satisfying.

Le Chevrier. One day while the writer was sketching in the quaint little town of Porto Maurizio on the Italian Riviera, Heintzelman came by, plate in hand, in quest of subject matter. He found it around the next corner and in an incredibly short space of time was back, "Le Chevrier" completed. But little work was subsequently added, and the whole breathes that spontaneity and freedom which only comes with depth of feeling and sureness of execution. The sun was hot and bright, that spring day in Italy, and the artist has filled his plate with its radiance. The pose of the goat herd and the arrangement of his charges, all leading up to the deep shadow of the arch in the background, are highly successful.

Arthur Wm. Heintzelman

Le Gamin de Borgio. One of the artist's finest portraits of children. Italy is full of just such delightful youngsters, but this particular one, in the little village perched high on its hill overlooking the Mediterranean, was especially amenable, and furnished a perfect subject for the exercise of Heintzelman's skill. There is great freedom in the modeling of the head, and a charming simplicity of execution, yet the portraiture is impeccable. The texture of the hair and of the lightly suggested shirt is very convincing, and the body and hands are admirably felt. Here we have a maximum of expression with a minimum of means, one of the most potent secrets of the etcher's art.

Arthur Wm. Heintzelman.

Merci. In this plate is realized a typical Parisian personality, an old musician who has sung his song and played his guitar, and is now about to collect a few sous for the pleasure he has given. This is of what may roughly be defined as Heintzelman's "middle period," if the work of such a young artist can, as yet, be so divided. The drawing is less precise than in the earlier plates and yet not so free as in the Italian subjects of 1926. The textures are beautifully rendered, and the pose of the body, with its slight stoop, is graceful yet firm. Here, as everywhere in Heintzelman's work, the line is clear cut and the forms well defined, with a total absence of any undue reliance upon the printing to achieve the desired result.

Heintzelman
Páris '22

Arthur Wm. Heintzelman